*Ouvriers français — les seuls auprès desquels je me
sente bien, que j'ai envie de connaître et de 'vivre.'
Ils sont comme moi.*

Carnets, mai 1935-fevrier 1942.

ALBERT CAMUS and the Men of the Stone

Edited by Robert Proix
Translated by Gregory H. Davis

The Greenwood Press 1971

Translator's Introduction

Who was Albert Camus? If we said he was a Frenchman born in French Algeria, a writer who was awarded the Nobel Prize for Literature in 1957, a leading journalist of the Resistance and early postwar period in France, and a famous existentialist 'philosopher of the absurd' who died absurdly in an automobile accident in 1960, we would expect no one to dispute our statements. But what did Camus really stand for? What was his ideological cast, his significance as a writer and thinker? What kind of man was he? Questions like these frequently lead us into the realm of ignorance and controversy — the horizon blurs, assertions are made, and tempers may flare up. We find ourselves fighting over the corpse of Camus.

Here in the United States, Camus enjoyed a certain vogue during the 1950's and early 1960's, particularly among college students and intellectuals. Although the enthusiasm of new writers and poets in France for Camus is restrained, a recent opinion poll indicated that he is the most popular writer among French students. He also has a strong following today with intellectuals in Latin America and Eastern Europe. The French Left, of course, claimed Camus as one of its most articulate spokesmen during World War II and the years immediately following the Liberation. Publication of *The Rebel* in 1951 and Camus' vacillating position on the war in Algeria, however, contributed to his condemnation by leading leftist intellectuals like Jean-Paul Sartre, Francis Jeanson, and their supporters inside and outside France. A Soviet publication derisively referred to Camus as 'the little Christ' after *The Rebel* appeared. His standing with the French Left was further degraded after he quipped to a journalist who asked him about the war in Algeria in 1957: 'If I had to choose between justice and my mother, I'd prefer my mother.' (Not only was French Algeria Camus' mother country, but his mother was still living there). The same disenchantment with Camus had set in among some American intellectuals by the late 1960's. John Gerassi, an American radical and expert on Latin America who taught at San Francisco State in 1968, angrily referred to Camus as the 'hero' of many well-meaning but ineffectual liberal intellectuals in the United States.

Even his personal life did not escape attack. In her novel *The Mandarins*, Simone de Beauvoir portrays the character Henri, obviously based on Camus, as a man with an excessive weakness for attractive women. What we conclude from this depends on whether we consider the characterization more revealing of Camus' or of Miss de Beauvoir's idiosyncrasies and whether we are prepared to forget that the novelist's craft often consists of embroidering fiction over fact. Camus, himself, in any case, ironized superbly over his reputation as a 'saint' in *The Fall*, published a few years before his death. Thus Camus was not without faults, nor critics and detractors.

In this short book, men of the stone — typographers, linotype operators, and proofreaders — have their say about Camus. For them, the preparation of this book was a matter of great importance, perhaps even a necessity. Robert Proix, the editor of this book in France, told the translator that he and his colleagues considered Camus 'irreplaceable.' This, of course, says a lot. These workers of the printing trades knew Camus personally, and it is obvious that they liked, respected, and admired him. They instinctively sensed that he, like they, had some printer's ink in his veins. In most cases they were more familiar, however, with Camus the man than with Camus the philosopher. Their words are simple and perceptive; the book is direct and unpretentious, faithful in tone and spirit to the man described in its pages. It is a warm human document.

By his very origins, Albert Camus couldn't help but be close to these men. His father, a mason, died the year after

8

Albert's birth, in the First Battle of the Marne. His mother, born on the island of Minorca and illiterate all her life, worked as a cleaning woman to support Albert and his brother. Camus grew up in Belcourt, a poor, working class quarter of Algiers. In 1948 he said: 'I didn't learn about freedom by reading Marx. The truth is that I learned from living in poverty.' Camus was able to continue his studies beyond the age of eleven only because of a scholarship, and he was forced to abandon graduate studies at the University of Algiers because he had been stricken with tuberculosis at the age of seventeen.

Some of us who have read Camus automatically associate him with the Mediterranean. Camus the Greek, we say, Camus the sensualist. We remember *The Stranger* and Meursault, the protagonist of the novel, who finds his destiny under the blazing Algerian sun. We recall the splendid essays about Algeria, where Camus describes almond trees in blossom, the fragrant Mediterranean landscape, and how as a boy he would warm himself against the stones of Roman ruins at Tipasa. We have in mind his 'sense of measure,' his cool irony, his abhorrence of romanticism and excess so apparent in *The Rebel* and so close to classical Mediterranean thought.

In this book, however, we see Camus in a world spiritually and sensually remote from the Mediterranean. He is in a France that has been defeated, humiliated, and occupied by the Germans; a France unable to revitalize itself at the war's end, unable to discover new ideals and a renewed sense of community. We see Camus existing, living, working in those metropolitan centers of Europe which he derided for their 'obsession with history.' We know he had little admiration for them, Paris included. Why else would he have referred contemptuously to Hegel as a *'philosophe des grandes villes'*? The workers of the printing trades who tell us here about Camus knew him when he was living away from the Mediterranean sun, in 'the night of Europe,' as he said in his essay, 'Return to Tipasa.'

Although this book contains primarily anecdotes and ex-

9

periences, there is a smattering of ideas relevant to the problems of contemporary America, particularly in the remarks made by Camus at a conference organized by the Proofreaders' Union. One of the subjects discussed at that meeting was the lack of communication between intellectuals and workers. American radicals, including militant groups like Students for a Democratic Society (SDS), have been painfully aware of this problem in the last few years. How do those who espouse critical philosophies and controversial ideals get their position across to the so-called 'silent majority,' working men and women who have been culturally starved and intellectually brutalized and are easily manipulated by the special interests and politicians who have ready access to the mass media? Some radicals have voiced the opinion that unless students and intellectuals can forge closer bonds with the American working class (besides minority group members), no significant political and social changes will ever be made in this country. At one point Camus suggests 'people's universities' as a possible solution to the problem of poor communication between workers and intellectuals. The 'free universities' organized in some parts of the United States in the 1960's have all eventually ended up with a middle class orientation and clientele, often serving only as a parallel institution designed to give dissatisfied college students some alternative to the multiversity, or as social mixers for unhappy bourgeois 'straights' who want to discover the delights and style of psychedelia. Why not establish some real 'people's universities,' designed along the lines Camus suggested, to provide some real intellectual enrichment and political culture for the American *workers*? Perhaps schemes to 'open' college campuses to the people, attempted in the United States with very limited success during the Cambodian crisis of spring, 1970, should be pursued more energetically.

Camus also mentioned the breakdown of belief in traditional social and national myths and the loss of a sense of community in modern society. The bitter antagonism between generations here in the United States as well as in other parts of the world is a graphic illustration of both problems. The old, broken in by habit and renunciation, still render homage to the forms of patriotism, security, and the duties of consumption; but the young reject these values. What new and satisfactory ideal can modern man live for, around what concepts or goals can he organize a meaningful life? One answer to these questions, or perhaps a means of rendering them superfluous, can be found in Camus' existential philosophy. At the proofreaders conference, Camus discusses the possibility of building a nonrepressive socialistic society. This, of course, might be a valid alternative to the welfare-warfare state represented by many of the leading industrialized nations. Certainly this concern for a humane form of socialism is not far from the goal of some members of the New Left and some of those individuals participating in commune experiments in the United States.

The remarks of Camus quoted in this book, like his writings in *The Rebel*, show him to be closer to the anarchist socialist than to the Bolshevik socialist tradition. Furthermore, just as he rejected the vicious cycle of terrorism and repression in the French-Algerian conflict, Camus refused to sanction a Soviet revolutionary morality based on the vulgar doctrine that the end justifies any and all means. This dilemma of means — both strategy and tactics — is the exact problem confronting American radicals today. To what extent should violence be used to change a corrupt society, and how can those who resort to violence avoid the inevitable backlash of repression, tolerated and even encouraged by a confused populace? How many American radicals, if they did succeed in seizing political power, would be willing to carry out a bloody repression of their own? It is obvious, in any case, that morality rather than history defined the limits of Camus' activism. It is precisely this stance which has made Camus unpopular with some contemporary radicals. They find Camus' sense of measure, his dislike for abstractions, his need for the concrete, and even his sensuality, inconvenient. Camus did not 'write in a dark closet,' like Thomas Hobbes, nor was he a *'machine à penser,'* an epithet one would sometimes like to apply to his country-man Jean-Paul Sartre.

Is Camus still contemporary, ten years after his death? It is tempting to try to situate his ideas midway along that radical segment of the American political and social spectrum fashionably described today as the 'counter-culture.' If the two poles of the counter-culture are the Mao-quoting militant revolutionaries of the New Left who aim to transform America by a violent revolution and the hippies and flower children who desire to transform society by a love explosion, it is apparent that Camus' place is not there. True, Camus wanted socialism; true also, he readily became a political activist when he joined the Resistance to combat Nazi tyranny. But there were practical and theoretical limits, as we have already seen, to his political commitment. Similarly, his tribute to Eros and the senses in early works like *The Stranger, The Myth of Sisyphus*, and the essays in *Nuptials* and *Summer* (both published in the American edition, *Lyrical and Critical Essays*, Alfred A. Knopf, 1968) was tempered by reason. Camus would not have been interested in the artificial paradise of psychedelia, buttressed with drugs, strobe lights, and incense. Camus was a Mediterranean man, and for him the beauties of nature and the joys of the senses were sufficient in themselves. Thus he was neither a political nor a sensual extremist, and this stance may place him at too many removes from contemporary American radicals. The nation's problems may be too extreme, the people's premonitions too apocalyptic. Perhaps Camus' thought is alienated from our problems — or are we alienated from it?

In the final analysis, however, Camus reserved his greatest respect for man and his willingness to confront the absurd and even transcend it by a kind of Nietzschean 'yea-saying' to the world. This respect flowed also toward individual men, for Camus' realm was of the heart — he was unwilling to hate.

This may be the reason why these workers of the printing trades, comrades of Camus, so readily and instinctively were drawn to him. They sensed his humanity; they knew he was authentic. And they shared his ideal that man's dignity ultimately had to be founded on every man's humanity and authenticity. Isn't that what the youth of today really want—to be human, and real?

Gregory H. Davis
Palo Alto, California

Acknowledgments
I would like to thank Mr. Jerome Tarshes, who read and edited the manuscript and made numerous useful suggestions. I am grateful to my wife, Hélène Laroche Davis, for helping with the translation on many occasions, and to Mr. Michael Taylor, for reading the manuscript and making helpful criticisms. Special thanks must be given to Madame Albert Camus for her aid in obtaining reproductions of photographs and other materials in France. Finally, without the constant support, interest, and assistance of Mr. Robert Proix, completion of an English version of this book would not have been possible. Mr. Proix provided useful background information concerning the Frenchmen who prepared the original edition and furnished valuable assistance in obtaining reproductions of photographs and illustrations from France.
G.H.D.

Albert Camus in his office at *Combat*, 1944.

Foreword

I have several misgivings in adding these words at the head of a homage which is the work of men of the stone, typographers and proofreaders. Between them and Albert Camus, there was a feeling of camaraderie that needed no intermediary. I was a witness to this for a few short years, in the composing room of Combat.[1] *Most of the men who describe in this book what working with Albert Camus was like were there.*

There are different kinds of journalists. Some of them have never set foot in the composing room. In my opinion, this is a mistake on their part. Camus first was a copy editor. When he became editor-in-chief, he continued to look after the make-up of each page, to check the final page proofs, and to wait at night for the completion of the page forms, which the 'truck' carried away, one after another. In conclusion, I think the printing plant was one of the places where Camus was happy.

When I learned of Camus' death,[2] I happened to be in the building at the Rue Reaumur, where previously the adventure of Combat *had begun. The first thing that I did was to go to the composing room, with Touratier, Georges Roy, and Lenief.[3] We felt the same grief.*

Reading these pages written by our comrades, I immediately recognized attitudes and images of Camus. Many speak of his smile. Those who wrote this book are men who haven't forgotten that smile.

Roger Grenier[4]

---

1. *Combat* was a clandestine news sheet published by French Resistance elements starting in December 1941. Camus began contributing articles to the paper in late 1943, and he joined the editorial staff in the spring of 1944. He became editor-in-chief in August of that year.
2. On January 4, 1960, Camus was killed in an automobile accident in the *département* of Yonne, roughly 70 miles southeast of Paris.
3. All three men were typographers.
4. Roger Grenier is a journalist and critic who worked with Camus at *Paris-Soir* and *Combat*.

Albert Camus and the Men of the Stone

A few workers in the printing trades got together to tape-record some memories of their association with Albert Camus. Here is the substance of their remarks.

Lemoine

formerly a typographer at *Paris-Soir*
and presently a proofreader at the *Figaro*:

I met Albert Camus in August 1940,[1] in Lyons. With *Paris-Soir*[2] we had first shifted to Clermont-Ferrand,[3] then to Lyons. It was there that I worked with Camus. I had the night shift, and Camus was at the composing stone the same hours as I. What a charming and agreeable guy! Simple and straight-forward, he was open to all criticisms concerning page make-up. If you told him what he wanted was impossible for technical reasons, he immediately acquiesced in a very nice way and everything would work out for the best.

He got married around the end of 1940 or the beginning of 1941, I believe.[4] Anyway, it was winter — the weather, as I recall, was pretty bad. Four of us, who were buddies, attended the wedding: Lemaître, Cormier, Lionet and myself. Maybe Lenief was there too.[5] We gave the newlyweds a bunch of violets. There was a very warm atmosphere. His wife was so pleasant! I'm sure she hasn't changed. I believe it was his second marriage, although we didn't know it at the time. In any case, when we left Paris together with *Paris-Soir*, we thought he was single. Rirette Maîtrejean made the trip with him, if I remember correctly.

1. France fell to the German invaders in June 1940.
2. Camus worked as a copy editor and refused to contribute any articles to *Paris-Soir* because of the political line of the paper.
3. Clermont-Ferrand is an industrial city in the mountainous region of central France, located approximately 240 miles south of Paris.
4. Camus' first marriage, in 1933, ended in divorce a year later. His second marriage to Francine Faure, which is mentioned here, took place in December 1940.
5. Lemaître was a linotype operator. Lenief, Cormier, and Lionet were typographers.

Rirette Maîtrejean
a retired proofreader:

That's correct. I met him at *Paris-Soir*, where he was a copy editor and I was a proofreader. We would run into one another at the composing stone and often talk while waiting for a page proof to be revised. But in that huge plant on the Rue du Louvre which housed our printing press, we never had a chance to get to know each other.

When everything collapsed, the paper withdrew first to Clermont-Ferrand, then to Lyons. They chose among the employees a handful of writers, several printers, a few more from the administrative staff, and evacuated us along those sinister roads. We were reunited there, a small group brought together by exile and the bitterness of the times. I don't know how we got on the subject, but one day Camus and I were discussing a book by Victor Serge,[1] an old friend of mine. He told me how much he liked the work of Victor Serge, and asked me a lot of questions about him. He was better at listening than at talking about himself. That's how we became friends.

He liked to hang around the composing stone with the typographers, who liked him. He was friendly and slightly ironic at the same time, always a charming comrade. We didn't know then that he was already an influential writer,

---

1. Victor Serge (born Victor Lvovich Kibalchick of Russian exile parents in Brussels) was a journalist, author, translator, and adherent to anarchist principles. Editor of the journal *l'Anarchie* in France, he returned to Russia for the Revolution. He became a member of the Trotskyite opposition, was exiled to Serbia, fled to France, and died in Mexico in 1947, a bitter opponent of all kinds of totalitarianism. His principal works about the Soviet Union are *From Lenin to Stalin* and *Russia Twenty Years After*; his novels include *The Long Dusk* and *The Case of Comrade Tulayev*. Rirette Maîtrejean was his companion when he edited *l'Anarchie*.

although we did realize that he was cut out for something bigger than what he was doing.

We took advantage of the small amount of gasoline and three or four automobiles we had among us to get away occasionally, to find some fresh air and a little more to eat than our horrible daily rations. I particularly remember an excursion we made to the summit of Puy de Dôme.[1] We stayed there quite a while, playing like children. Then we had a marvelous country meal at a little village inn where Camus, sometimes comical and charming, sometimes melancholy and very human, made it a lively occasion. From my end of the table I listened to him pensively. I knew that he would have to leave us in a few days, and that evening I was bitterly sad about it. Our comrade Lemoine has already described Camus' marriage during his stay in Lyons and how our buddies, typographers, served as witnesses for the ceremony. That's how close he was to us.

Later I ran into him again in Paris, at a meeting of the editorial committee of *Témoins,*[2] a review to which he sometimes contributed. He was already famous, but he was still as simple and friendly as ever. On that particular day he did me a great favor, in fact without my even having to ask for it. He had a kind of sixth sense for what was good or necessary. Afterwards I occasionally visited him at Gallimard,[3] where his friendship was precious to me. After you had chatted with him for fifteen minutes, life seemed a little more bearable. You left feeling comforted, more able to put up with the human race.

How miserable Fate sometimes is! I'm already an old woman, without strength or courage. There are thousands of us like that, spending most of our time by the fireside, devouring books, listening to a little music, people perfectly use-

1. Puy de Dôme is a peak 4,800 feet high and is located six miles west of Clermont-Ferrand.
2. *Témoins* is a quarterly literary review of anarchist tendency, founded in 1952 by Jean-Paul Samson and edited in Zurich.
3. Gallimard is one of the most important publishing houses in France.

less but living. And he, with his marvellous intelligence, his unbounded potential, his youth, he's gone.

Yes, he's gone, carrying away with him a part of our lives. I still can't believe it. Since that frightful day, every time I set foot in Gallimard I take little looks, right and left, in the small hall and in the long corridors, expecting him to appear suddenly from around a corner. I keep thinking that all I have to do is climb up to the third floor, knock on a door, and open it to see his warm smile and handsome, kind face.

The figure of Albert Camus towers over us. I don't know how to talk about him in a right way, as I would have liked. But the memory of his friendship will always be a comfort to me.

Georges Roy

a typographer at the newspaper *France-Soir*:

I met Albert Camus during the Liberation, at *Combat*. It was
the month of August 1944, when the paper began publishing
openly. Camus was no longer only a journalist, but director
and editor-in-chief as well; and we were able to appreciate his
talents completely. I was a workers' representative. We had
to deal with Camus concerning specific problems connected
with the Liberation. On these matters we found him extraor-
dinary. Right away he understood the most complicated
matters, the various problems of the workers which I had out-
lined — and they were pretty tricky. Camus understood; he
really was one of the boys in the composing room, someone
you could consider a worker in the printing trades. He had
picked up our particular way of doing things, our vocabulary,
our virtues and our shortcomings. He was at home in the
composing room, full of high spirits, a great kidder, and always in on the joke — in short, he really fitted in.

He was extremely understanding concerning salaries and
new working conditions, and nothing stalled once he took it
in hand. At that time he had great hopes. You could tell from
his editorials, from talking to him, that he thought something
new was in the air, that something had changed, that we were
on the threshold of a period where men would change for the
better. But the day he left *Combat*[1] (we were together at the
composing stone), I had the impression he was disillusioned.
He had hoped that men had learned some lessons from the war

1. Plagued by ailing health, financial difficulties, and disagreement with pro-
Gaullist editorialists Pascal Pia, Raymond Aron, and Albert Ollivier over the
paper's political line, Camus announced his resignation from *Combat* on June 3,
1947. Henri Samdja, a rich Tunisian with socialist leanings, bought the paper; and
Claude Bourdet, a journalist and intellectual of the Left, took over as editor-in-
chief.

and the occupation. He gave me the feeling he was saying to himself: 'All that was no use at all. We have to start over again, at the beginning. Nothing has changed.' He got out of journalism at that time and stepped back into the shadows after *Combat*. It wasn't until much later that we found him back in the composing room, this time when the *Express* appeared on the newsstands.[1] I realized that after two years of militant journalism with *Combat*, despite his editorials, despite the controversy with *Figaro* (those were the days when he kept up a running dialogue with François Mauriac[2]), he thought that 'it hadn't made any difference.' When we said goodbye in the bar, I said to him, 'You seem to have been quite disappointed.' As a matter of fact, he was.

Up to that time he had spoken much more from the heart than with his pen. He had cultivated friendship and understanding: our relationship was living proof of this. He was always even-tempered; I never saw him get angry, even when things weren't going his way. He was always calm and warm-hearted. He was delighted when we called him 'Albert' and addressed him by the familiar *tu*. He was a friend, and you could be completely open with him. And he never changed. Remember when our friend Jacques published a book?[3] Camus was very nice to him and gave him some helpful advice. When Camus received the Nobel Prize, I sent him a congratulatory note. Here's what he wrote in return:

1. At the time, the *Express* was a leftist newspaper published by Jean Jacques Servan-Schreiber. Today it is published as a weekly news magazine with a *Time* format. Camus began writing for the *Express* in May of 1955.
2. François Mauriac was a Catholic intellectual, journalist, and novelist (*Thérèse Desqueyroux*.) In his column in the *Figaro* he took issue with Camus for his uncompromising insistence on harsh sentences for collaborators during the French purge trials which began in 1944.
3. Jacques was a typographer at *Paris-Presse*. He was brought up in an orphanage and later wrote an autobiography, *Moi Jacques sans nom* (*I, Jacques No-name*).

24 November 1957

Thanks with all my heart, dear Roy, both to you and to our comrade, for your words of friendship. Honors are worth what they are worth, and also what the men who give them are worth. But I'll always be proud to have kept the esteem and friendship of men like you, who worked for a long time at the same composing stone as I. I shake hands with both of you in friendship.

Albert Camus

Working with us at *Combat* was Cordier,[1] who unfortunately is no longer alive. Cordier would have been able to give us many details concerning his relationship with Camus. Whenever they made up a page together, there were long conversations, and they never ran out of things to talk about.

I have to admit we started the newspaper, on August 19th, without knowing how anyone was going to be paid or anything else. In the beginning there hadn't been any real discussion about salaries among the editorial writers, the management, and ourselves. No one left the plant; we ate and slept there. Everyone was preoccupied with getting out the newspaper. As far as other matters were concerned, they had to wait until later. But the atmosphere was alive and friendly, and we all got along marvelously. Touratier, the number-two man, worked with Cordier. Camus liked to call him 'Bebert.'[2] Later they corresponded with each other. Here's a letter from Camus to Touratier:

28 August

Dear Touratier,
It would be difficult for me to tell you how deeply your letter touched me. I'm far away from Paris and Combat, *which I left with a heavy heart over a year ago now. That's why this anniversary didn't go by without sorrow. I also reread my first editorial — not without sadness, believe me. Together we signed it with our work,*

1. He was a typographer.
2. 'Bebert' is a nickname for Albert.

our struggle, and the hopes we shared. But we were at a disadvantage because we were honest. The press, which we wanted to be proud and worthy of its name, is today the disgrace of this unhappy country. But at least something endured; your letter proves it to me. I'm referring to the fraternal bonds that a handful of men forged out of their daily toil and the danger they shared.

Thank you, dear Touratier, thanks to all of you for thinking of me on that particular day. I, too, am proud that we stood side by side during those difficult times. I haven't forgotten the risks each of you had to take so you could be at the composing stone, where we set in type our highest hopes. Nor have I forgotten the simplicity with which you accomplished that difficult task. What joy, how moved I am, to know that I have been able to keep your goodwill and remain in your thoughts! This is why I never give up hope. Perhaps there will come a day when we'll be able to work and fight together again. In the meantime, I send you fraternal greetings and I wish you and your families the best of luck from the bottom of my heart.

Albert Camus

P.S. Tell me, confidentially, what our comrade[1] who worked on the clandestine edition of Combat needs and how I can help him

'Paterne'[2]
Isle-sur-Sorgue
Vaucluse

We spent two years of our lives like this in the company of Camus, without friction or quarrels, in perfect friendship. Later I went to see him at the N.R.F.[3] He was very nice. He still was friendly to the profession and the men of the printing trades.

---

1. It is not clear to whom Camus was referring, unless it was Touratier himself who was asking for a favor.
2. Literally, this means 'the benevolent one.'
3. The *Nouvelle Revue Française* (N.R.F.) was one of the most progressive and influential literary reviews in France. Started before World War I, it increased in prestige under the editorship of André Gide and with the financial backing of Gallimard. Camus' job with the N.R.F. was to screen manuscripts and make recommendations to the editor.

Camus in the composing room
of the daily newspaper, *Express*, 1955.

Les Barricades de la Rue Sèvestre et de la Rue d'Orsel

The Paris insurrection seen by a witness:
Barricades at Rue Sèvrestre & Rue d'Orsel, 1944.

Lamaître
a linotype operator and secretary of the *Comité d'entreprise*[1]
at the newspaper *Aurore*:

As far as I'm concerned, the image I've retained of Albert
Camus is that of a perfect comrade. We accepted him right
from the start, something quite rare. We had many problems
in Lyons. The Lyonnais, who hadn't been very cooperative in
the beginning, gave the Parisians the cold shoulder. When
Camus set foot in the composing room, however, right away
there was a ray of sunlight. He was a real live wire, wasn't
stuck-up, and fit in right from the start. We really liked that.
We had the impression we'd known him for years. Always
ready for a joke, he was a comedian among us. When we sang
merry songs, no one had to wait for him to join in on the
chorus. He had a repertory of barrack songs — not the kind
you could sing around your family, of course, but very enter-
taining.

He really impressed us on his wedding day. I was touched
by the way he got married — so simple, with three or four
typographers as the wedding procession. What proof of his
friendship that was for us! His wife was so unpretentious, so
nice. When we left the City Hall,[2] we all went to a café, like
buddies getting together.

We knew that he loved the atmosphere of the printing
plant. He liked to have the pages and galleys of type in front
of him. He was literally hooked on the printer's craft. It's true
that there's a kind of intoxication in it: the odor of printer's
ink and damp paper — you love to smell it, the way a leather

1. This means, literally, 'committee of the enterprise.' The committees, estab-
lished at the end of the war, were composed of delegates elected by workers in each
factory. Intended to give workers a greater sense of participation and control, they
actually had only the power to make recommendations to the management
concerning working conditions and fringe benefits.
2. In France, the civil ceremony takes place in the city hall (*mairie*).

worker loves to smell the odor of leather. Camus spent more time at the composing room than in the editorial offices. And remember that he never signed his editorials. That was something really unusual — you never saw his signature at the bottom of an editorial. He really didn't want to be in the limelight.

I saw him again a few times when *Paris-Presse* was getting started. It was a pleasure to shake hands with him, for he never took on the superior airs of someone who had to be addressed 'Mister'; you said 'hello, Albert' or 'hello, Camus,' just as you would to anyone else you worked with. Naturally, we pretty much lost sight of him when he became a famous writer. We used to talk about him among ourselves. Occasionally someone suggested writing to ask him a favor, but we didn't dare. We thought the demands of his work and personal affairs were sufficient, and we were afraid of wasting his time. When the catastrophe occurred, I was very sorry I had gone so long without looking him up. The image that I will always have of Camus is that of a perfect comrade.

Pierre Blin

a linotype operator at the *Figaro* and
one of the team which had worked on
the clandestine edition of *Combat*:

I was a member of the Oise[1] partisan group when Paris was
liberated. I still remember very clearly a conversation I had
with Camus at that time. Since the paper subsequently would
be coming out legally, we had reconstituted the *Comité
d'entreprise*. But what kind of enterprise would it be? Were we
only going to change bosses? This wasn't the goal we had
worked for during the course of all our clandestine activities.
I told Albert Camus that in view of the circumstances, it was
absolutely necessary to set up a workers' cooperative. He told
me he agreed completely. Unfortunately, the proposal was
opposed by an active minority, and it failed. Camus had ex-
pected as much and let me know how he felt. I can see why he
saw dark days ahead. If everyone had been made of the same
stuff as he was, the prospects would have been different.

1. This is a district just north of Paris.

Maurice Leroy
a typographer at the *Figaro*

It was in 1943, when *Combat* was printed underground in Lyons and edited secretly in Paris. One day Girard (now with *Paris-Jour*) informed me that the editorial team of *Combat* had been spotted, more or less, and they were looking for a new place to hold meetings. I immediately offered them my lodgings at the rue d'Aboukir. Shortly afterwards Albert Camus showed up at my place with the following people: Bloc-Michel, Pascal Pia, Albert Ollivier, Marcel Gimont, Altschuler, Coquelin, Jacqueline Bernard, and so on — in short, the entire editorial staff of *Combat*. Thanks to the co-operation of my concierge, Madame Simone, we were safe from possible dangers: we had a prearranged signal by which she would let us know about any unusual incidents.

I didn't realize then what Camus' strong personality would soon mean to all of us on the *Combat* team. Living among us in the most simple way, sharing the hazards of our daily exist-ence, Camus gave us the impression that he, too, was a worker; and we treated him just like one of the gang. What's more, he used the familiar *tu* with practically all of us.

Once the day when we could publish openly had come, Camus gave me the job of forming a team to print the paper in Paris. Georges Roy has already described the difficulties we had getting started and how the negotiation of our working conditions was made easier with Albert Camus there. That was something we'll always remember. Later, when we saw Camus' career go the way it did, all of us to a man were happy about it. When he received the Nobel Prize, I sent him a few words of congratulation. He replied with a note that I've held on to as one of my most precious possessions. It begins, 'Thanks, dear emperor . . .'.

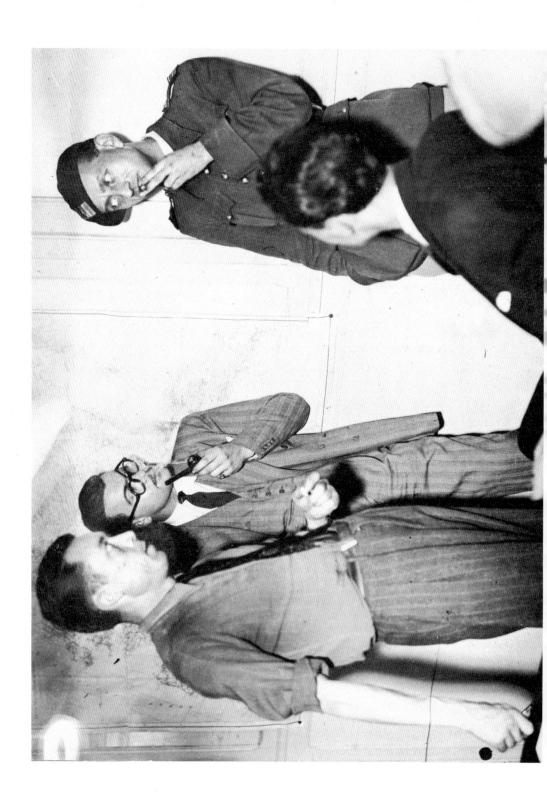

Camus, Jacques Baumel, and André Malraux
in the offices of *Combat*, 1944.

Those comrades who were one of us will remember that in the Underground my name, Leroy, had won me the nickname, given by Jacqueline Bernard, of 'the Emperor'; this explains the greeting used by Camus in his note.[1] Here is an example of the fellowship that incomparable man showed toward us over and over again.

You often hear us say that Camus was very disillusioned after negotiations with *la Voix du Nord* failed, Claude Bourdet and Samdja joined the paper, and he found himself obliged to give up *Combat*. This wasn't my impression. It seemed to me, on the contrary, he accepted that necessity with a certain sense of relief, since he hadn't been able to carry out his original plan of turning the paper into a really free forum, where the most controversial ideas of the time would clash head on. This concept was too original and undoubtedly cannot be implemented in a time like ours.

Be that as it may, the majority of us were convinced by then that Camus was incontestably superior to the other journalists and writers. And his name eventually became well-known. I have in mind an anecdote which will give you an idea of what I mean. When the French prizefighter Halimi beat his American opponent, the public was very impressed. One sportswriter decided to stop people at random in the streets, cafés, and public places and ask them who, in their opinion, was the greatest Frenchman at that moment. Needless to say, many people answered 'Halimi!' But one waiter in a café on the Champs-Elysées exclaimed spontaneously, to the great surprise of the reporter, 'Albert Camus!'

1. Leroy is a derivative from *le roi*, which means 'the king.'

Daniel Lenief
an editor at *France-Soir*:

I met Camus the day he joined *Paris-Soir*, at the beginning of the war. He was received by the editor-in-chief of the paper, and I still remember the end of their conversation.[1]

'We don't get involved in politics here,' said the editor. Camus replied, very calmly, 'Of course not!'

He, Henri Coquelin, and myself were assigned to the copy desk; we made up a team. We hadn't known him very long before he won us over completely, and the rapport we felt at first quickly turned into friendship.

The days passed without any disagreements, at least as far as we were concerned. Then came the evacuation. We were supposed to drive to Clermont-Ferrand in automobiles which had been turned over to us because almost all of the regular drivers had been mobilized. We were the first to arrive, and I can still see Camus, getting out of a smoking car on Jaude Square, out of gas, oil, and water. He turned pale, rushed to the rear trunk, and took out, as if it were a treasure, a manuscript which he buried in his pockets. I later learned it was the manuscript for *The Stranger*, which he thought he had left behind. Then his anxiety vanished, and he told us with great humor how the executive riding with him had managed to sustain all night a conversation that flagged at times because of his drowsiness.

During our stay at Clermont-Ferrand, each of us did his own cooking. But occasionally Camus came to share our scanty meals in a tiny room where my brother, who had joined us, prepared the food and where two other comrades were boarders. On the days of these 'receptions,' we invited

1. Camus wasn't sympathetic with the pro-German line of *Paris-Soir*. See p.21, n. 2.

him to come and stand in line with us at the stores before lunch; and his sarcastic comments made the long waiting seem short.

One evening the young people of the region were celebrating Saint John's Eve[1] in the mountains, and we went to watch them. Camus was with us, and all the way back — it was a bright night — he entertained us with marching songs. But they weren't all so gay; you can judge by a few lines from one of them.

> *Born on the Day of the Dead,*[2]
> *Wasn't that a fate so sad?*
> *Seduced by three on the Trinity,*
> *That was a calamity.*[3]

Wasn't that enough to make you cry? Believe me, it wasn't, because we had a good laugh.

After our stay at Clermont-Ferrand we all went to Lyons, where Camus had to leave us several months later. The exact date escapes me, but I can still remember the lunch with his wife, Coquelin, and myself. He was completely relaxed, and at that little gathering the four of us were like one family. A few moments before we broke up, he said to me in a matter-of-fact way: 'I'll be counting on you in Paris the day of the Liberation.' When that day arrived, I was still in Lyons, working for a Resistance paper. I left to join Camus at *Combat*, where he was waiting for me, just like he said he would be.

Already, in such a brief period of time, his editorials had created a sensation. François Mauriac, at the *Figaro*, had found in Camus a worthy adversary and felt obliged to answer his editorials in a kind of dialogue where they equalled each other

1. Midsummer's Eve, June 23.
2. All Souls' Day, November 2.
3. *Elle était née le Jour des Morts*
   C'est un bien triste sort
   Elle fut séduite a la Trinité
   C'est une calamité.

in nobility of thought and beauty of style. The whole press still remembers this.

His rapid rise hadn't changed him. He still had the same goodwill towards us. No matter what we asked for, Camus invariably gave us a favorable response within a few hours. The director at the time, Bloch-Michel, was a comrade and always gave the final O.K.

And then, for reasons of health, he had to leave his paper, which he and Pascal Pia had managed together.[1] There was a period of transition and uncertainty, and then he returned only to give up *Combat*, after he had put so much of himself into it. That was practically over his dead body. Why? Because he wanted to protect at any cost the jobs of those who had worked with him. They had relied on him, and he had never let them down. Go ask the workers in the printing trade who knew him what they think of him. All the ones who are still around will tell you, with words straight from the heart, what a great guy he was.

His career as a journalist had to end there. After that I went to see him at his apartment. One day he sadly confided to me his anguish when one of the persons who had admired him the most grew distant and when a former co-worker whom he had helped get ahead took a job with a newspaper that continually smeared him. That was the only time I heard him express his resentment, which must have been considerable!

Fortunately, his retirement didn't last long. You must remember his dazzling literary career afterwards, his success in the theater, and finally his triumph with the Nobel Prize.[2] When he returned from Stockholm, I telephoned my congratulations, and this is more or less how the conversation went:

1. At the age of seventeen, Camus was stricken with tuberculosis, and he suffered from the after-effects of this illness for the rest of his life. Camus remained absent from *Combat* for almost a year, returning in November 1946.
2. Camus received the Nobel Prize for Literature in December 1957.

Camus in 1945 at the Paris sidewalk café 'Deux
Magots,' reading with mock seriousness a copy
of the Salvation Army newspaper.

OU SONT LES ASSASSINS ?

Parisians reading a poster concerning the
assassination of a collaborationist leader in June 1944.

'Bravo!'

'Thanks!'

'Say, you really look good in a cutaway!'

'So what? What do you take me for?'

And we never mentioned the Nobel Prize again.

I always kept in touch with him. I ran into him on several other occasions, and he hadn't changed a bit. Although our occupations had put some distance between us, in his heart he was still the same. His death was a terrible shock for me.

At the request of Robert Proix, I have given you a few random recollections. They don't pretend to present Camus covered with laurels, but rather to show him as a comrade, a friend in the fullest sense of the word. I hope I have succeeded!

Robert Proix
a retired proofreader:

Rirette put it very astutely when she said: 'The surprising
thing is that although he was completely at ease among the
workers, he didn't seem to be with the journalists. His career
as a journalist was short. Perhaps he was never accepted by
journalists the way we had adopted him.'

He had begun his newspaper career in Algiers, with a report
on conditions in the Kabylia region.[1] When his articles appeared, they brought him trouble — some people were dis-
pleased because he had revealed the misery in Kabylia. Thus
he had started out on the wrong foot. He wasn't much hap-
pier at *Combat* (Bourdet never failed to mention this afterwards). Camus wasn't free to say what he wanted. He wasn't
cut out for that kind of work. Writing an article in haste,
without revising or remaining true to the facts, was a task
bound to give him displeasure. Later he experienced a major
disappointment at the *Express*. Spontaneous and sometimes
enthusiastic, he had gone overboard for Mendès.[2] He had even
written a completely *engagé* article in the *Express*, and I told
him how much the article had surprised me. His illusions were

1. Kabylia is a rugged mountainous region in northern Algeria, between Algiers
and Constantine. In 1939 this region, which had a much higher population density
than most other parts of Algeria, suffered a terrible famine. Camus detailed the
miserable living conditions of its inhabitants and sharply criticised the indifference
and incompetence of French authorities in the area and the way French colonists
exploited the native population.
2. The *Express* became a daily paper in October 1955, in order to support Pierre
Mendès-France in the national elections. Mendès had allied his Radical Party with
the Socialists to form the non-communist but leftist *Front Républicain*, which ad-
vocated progressive and moderate reforms. Servan-Schreiber, the *Express'*
publishers, successfully persuaded Camus to support Mendès. From October to
December, when the elections were held, Camus submitted two articles a week.
Many of his editorials of this period dealt with the war in Algeria, however, including his famous but unproductive appeal for a truce on December 16, 1955.

shattered when he saw the direction French politics were going, even under Mendès. He didn't wait until the daily *Express* was discontinued to stop all work for that paper or for any other. When he joined us at the editorial offices of the review, *Témoins*, his capacity for enthusiasm had been considerably dulled. Nevertheless, he told us that he approved of our effort, and he helped out despite his tight schedule.

At any rate, he never broke off contact with those of us who continued to be, in a way, his liaison agents with his friends in the printing trades. That's how we got him to agree, toward the end of 1957, to appear before a study group organized by the Proofreaders' Union and present his views on what the relationship between writers and workers in the printing trades ought to be.

Here is a report[1] of that conference, which was an unforgettable experience both for those who planned it and those who participated:

Could we have hoped for a more productive exchange of views than one involving the man who symbolized, in our eyes, the finest expression of contemporary thought and the men whose profession was producing the material elements which make written works available to the general public?

It was an unusual audience and included, along with the proofreaders, who had come in large numbers, members of federated unions from all categories of the book and printing trades.

First Faucier[2] explained the topic that Camus had agreed to discuss. Then our comrade Lazarevich made, in a few moving words, the finest compliment you could possibly give a man: 'One thing is clear,' he said, 'we have with us one of

1. This resumé is based on notes taken by Mr. Proix at the conference and later approved by Albert Camus.
2. Faucier, a proofreader, was a militant anarchist and trade unionist. Imprisoned before 1930 for his political activities, he helped found *le Secours international anti-fascist*, an international organization which aided the Republican cause during the Spanish Civil War with funds collected in the unions.

those rare writers who refuses to be corrupted.'

Having thus created a sympathetic atmosphere, Lazarevich[1] laid down the ground rules for our encounter with Albert Camus. Basically, we could question our guest about what the relationship between the writer and workers in the printing trades should be. We were to avoid as much as possible, however, bringing up matters which Camus preferred not to discuss. Lazarevich suggested we keep certain facts in mind during our discussion: 1) we were living at a time when there were numerous obstacles to the dissemination of ideas; 2) science and technology, nevertheless, could only progress by means of the printing press; 3) and radio was able to overturn all kinds of conventions — for example, when it worked the miracle of letting us hear Camus read *Caligula* and thus provoked surprising response from young listeners.[2]

Often it's apparent, Lazarevich pointed out, that people are tired of slogans and stereotypes designed to anesthetize the masses' critical judgment. When, for example, *Literaturnaya Gazieta*,[3] in speaking of Camus and referring to *The Rebel*, calls him 'the little Christ,' it's obviously an attempt to ridicule the author and discourage people from reading the book.[4] Yet it's quite possible that somewhere, at Vorkuta[5] or elsewhere, an inquisitive person wanted, nevertheless, to find out what was in the book and to verify to what extent its meaning

1. Lazarevich was another anarchist militant and proofreader. Born in Russia, he was forced to leave the country after the Revolution because of his political views. He has been active among Russian émigré intellectuals in France who oppose the direction the Revolution took under Lenin and Stalin.
2. Surprising as it may seem today, in 1955 only .6 per cent of the French population had television sets. Thus radio was a more important medium for diffusing culture to the masses in the mid-fifties than it is today.
3. *Literaturnaya Gazieta* is the official weekly publication of the Soviet Writers' Union.
4. Soviet Marxists, and pro-Soviet French leftist intellectuals such as Jean-Paul Sartre and Francis Jeanson writing in *Les Temps Modernes*, criticised Camus in 1952 for his rejection of a revolutionary morality which justified *a priori* any and all excesses committed in the name of 'The Revolution,' at best a vague and abstract promise for a future utopia.
5. Vorkuta is a coal-mining town in the northern Urals, situated inside the Arctic Circle. In the early post-war period the forced-labor camps there had an estimated population of 500,000.

Albert Camus and his books, circa 1957.

Combat, No. 59, 21 August 1944, the day of the
liberation of Paris. Two articles appear on the
front page by Camus: 'De la Résistance a la Révolution'
and 'Le combat continue . . .'.

had been distorted. In that way someone will have been reached, in spite of the obstacles, and he will derive a moral lesson from what he has read. Thus, nothing is ever really finished, and that's why we should be able to draw some valuable conclusions from our meeting with Albert Camus.

Lazarevich concluded by extended a fraternal invitation to Camus to speak to us freely, from the heart.

With characteristic simplicity, Camus told us how he felt about the matter: certainly there was a separation, all too obvious, between workers and intellectuals; it was particularly unfortunate as far as workers in the printing trades were concerned. We had to try to bridge the gap.

The first question from the floor concerned the relationship between the writer and the proofreader. Camus assured us that, in his case, he gave full and friendly consideration to any suggestion made by the proofreader relative to meaning and syntax; furthermore, he said that eight out of ten times he followed the proofreader's advice. Thus their relations were perfectly courteous.

Then he broadened the discussion by sketching a picture for us of the writer's life in general and his own in particular. If sometimes people seemed to have to pull him by the ear to get him to attend this or that meeting, discussion, or social gathering, he said, it was because he had an incredibly busy schedule; moreover, he thought he couldn't create anything worthwhile without long hours of solitary meditation. After that there remained the physical labor, which consisted of writing out the work himself or dictating it.

It's well known that a writer has difficulty making a living from his books. He therefore needs a second occupation, unless he wants to sell popular novels or bread-and-butter articles. This second occupation absorbs him for hours and sometimes for several days each week. In addition, there is correspondence. Camus received 400 letters a month on the

49

average, and he made it a point to answer them. Finally, since he was both a playwright and a director, he devoted three months a year — day and night — to the theater. After that, what was left for his private life? 'And,' he said, 'regardless of what certain people think, I'm not a "little Christ"!'

His mission, you see, was to keep on writing and remain a kind of 'travelling salesman for a certain way of thinking.' How, under these conditions, could he maintain uninterrupted contact with the outside, with the world of labor? How could he find the means for this contact? How could he span the 'chasm' (this was Faucier's term) which has opened up between manual laborer and intellectual?

'I see the first step toward a solution in freedom of work and cultural freedom,' said Camus. 'But work today is slavery, and the intellectual has absolutely no freedom. Protecting the rights of labor is the same thing as defending the rights of intellectuals. Where else could these two groups find a common meeting ground, if not in the union? The workers' union is politicized, however; and as far as the writers' is concerned, it's nonexistent. How could it be created? By inviting intellectuals, as you have done today, to participate in discussions before study groups; by recreating 'people's universities.' But where are the militants, and what free time do they have? It's obvious that the intellectuals are silent and have no contact with what one might call a workers' movement, if one existed. For there isn't any workers' movement worthy of the name. How can we become part of a nonexistent movement? Certainly there's no shortage of problems which have to be discussed, but where are the points on which we can all agree? Invite us, provoke us into discussion. We'll do what we can.'

In response to a question concerning 'the social question,' Camus agreed this was a serious matter, which the writer should only approach cautiously. He had to avoid 'taking responsibility for the workers' lot' and turning out hackneyed works in the style of Ilya Ehrenburg, or becoming a 'boy-scout of social activism.' Without falling into the error of art for art's sake — a fundamental error — he was perfectly justified in discussing certain subjects prudently. But he should not lose sight of the fact that he writes to be read. Communication and solidarity with the society of men were necessary. He had to address himself, therefore, to the greatest number without letting this stifle his aspiration to create a work of art. Compare, for example, a Gide and a Tolstoy. We could say that the former contributed to a certain kind of liberation, although he was a perfect example of the man of letters who doesn't write for the people. Tolstoy, on the other hand, was a member of the landed gentry. He wrote works that were understood by all men and that have, nevertheless, all the qualities of a work of art.

'So, when I wrote "The Silent Men," a short story in *Exile and the Kingdom* about a strike in a barrel factory in Algiers,' Camus said, 'I felt very uneasy. I couldn't get the thought out of my mind that successfully describing a strike, or more precisely, its effects, in language that communicates is an extremely delicate undertaking. I hope I succeeded all the same!'

'In your capacity as a journalist,' someone said, 'haven't you ever been hampered by the political climate and by orders from your bosses?'

'Certainly the act of writing an editorial necessarily involves concessions, as much to public opinion as to colleagues who write in the same paper. This leads to saying less, rather than more. I have therefore never been satisfied working as a journalist: first, because this demands a speed of execution which always annoys me and makes it almost impossible to revise anything; second, because I abhor having enemies, and journalistic polemics invariably end up this way. I suffer perpetually for this reason. You have to admit we live here in the capital of systematic spitefulness, disparagement, and falsehood. We live continually in the midst of a miserable conspiracy which renders the atmosphere in this country practically unbearable. But what can we do about it?'

'A certain number of writers who are more or less influential,' said another person, 'are rather dogmatic. Isn't this dangerous?'

'We should recognize,' Camus replied, 'that in this historical period it's difficult to express yourself in a country like ours, one that exhibits acute signs of a decadence whose principal characteristics is a kind of atomization. Either we are highly aware of our solitude and the impossibility in our situation of committing ourselves to something — love, religion, society — or we delude ourselves by thinking we have some ideological affiliation. With that posture, for some, there were no more problems. The problems returned after the report of the Twentieth Congress.[1] What seems obvious to me is that we're all tired — the French generally and writers in particular. You can detect this in the ill humor of Parisians and the despair of people who live alone. But what can we believe in? There was a time when the Monarchy, or Christianity, offered men a kind of coherence. Today, what form of government or what form of ideology would be capable of bringing us together? Thus, the attitude of many French writers reflects a general attitude. Let's try to unite in the hope that all this can be changed. Let's try to be honest and learn how to avoid lying in our capacity as writers.'

Aubrée[2] maintained that the principal causes of this confusion and failure of intellect were the divorce between technological civilization and the labor movement, with the extreme centralization of power and the lack of responsibility which this produces.

'Here is where the two explanations coincide. Thanks to the Industrial Revolution, two tendencies have manifested

1. The reference, of course, is to the Twentieth Congress of the Communist Party of the Soviet Union, held in February 1956. Khrushchev made his famous secret speech, denouncing the crimes and excesses of the Stalinist era.
2. Aubrée was another worker present at the conference.

themselves in the world of labor. The first, revolutionary socialism — Proudhonian and populistic — was broken by History. The second, centralized and Cesarian socialism,[1] is unable to put the conquests of technology in proper balance. But the struggle between libertarian and Cesarian socialism isn't over, and there's no possibility that the first will make any compromise with the second. A good example is Scandinavian socialism, a clever junction of labor and management organisms. There, in effect, unions have complete autonomy, and it's possible to safeguard libertarian values within the union. We can say, in any case, that revolutions with machine guns at the street corners are finished there.'

Aubrée remarked, 'don't technocracy and present-day research, with the exception of investigation of libertarian possibilities, tend to reinforce the power of government over men?'

'That's why,' Camus replied, 'the rebirth of a non-partisan labor movement is indispensable. This is the only way a leadership elite can be formed inside the working class, since the lack of cadres is essentially a result of politicizing the labor movement. The problem is to build men through the union.'

Lazarevich, apparently changing the subject, asked Camus what kind of reception was accorded to his short story 'The Silent Men,' which he had mentioned previously. 'There wasn't,' Camus replied, 'a single letter from a working man, nor did any labor magazine ask permission to reprint it. As far as the book itself is concerned, it's obvious that it didn't sell very well among the workers. This was undoubtedly because books are too expensive.'

'Furthermore, your play, The Just Assassins, didn't have much impact. How can you explain that? It dealt, moreover, with important human problems, since it retraced an episode

1. By 'revolutionary socialism,' Camus meant the anarchist socialist tradition, which emphasizes worker ownership and control of the means of production and decentralized social, political, and economic institutions and processes. 'Centralized and Cesarean socialism,' on the other hand, refers to Soviet-type Marxism, which includes a repressive state and its bureaucratic mechanisms.

in the revolutionary struggle of 1905.'

'It's that the theater, like books, is too expensive, and besides, this is another manifestation of that fatigue of the entire nation which we were discussing a few minutes ago.'

'But even so,' someone remarked, 'the circus and the music hall, where seats are very expensive, play to a full house. And you see many working class families there.'

'I would feel guilty if I made any kind of reproach to working people who, tired after their week, have every right to find some kind of distraction.'

One of the workers observed that it was extremely difficult for the average wage-earner to decide on a course of action, confronted as he was with the attitude of a so-called 'intellectual Left' which was more determined to fight Marxism than capitalism.

'Personally,' said Camus, 'I energetically refuse to be considered a "guide of the working class." This is an honor I decline. There are lots of things I'm unsure about, and I constantly need to be enlightened. It's altogether too easy to decide from an office what a wage-earner should do — we all have our own problems.

'I may have been a communist, but I have never been a Marxist.[1] Certainly Marxism is still valid as a method for criticising bourgeois mystifications, just as any fertile idea or doctrine is valid. But let's beware of the Marxist schema without falling into any kind of apology for capitalism. Capitalist society is no longer what it was in the nineteenth century. Yet can we say that the society which calls itself socialist corresponds to its original definition? Let's preciously

---

1. Camus joined the Algerian Communist Party in 1934, when he was twenty-one years old and still a student. Camus himself claimed he resigned in May 1935, after Pierre Laval's visit to Moscow and the signing of the Franco-Soviet Pact, which resulted in a softening of the Algerian party's hostility to French colonial policies. Some of his associates claim he remained in the Party until 1937, when he allegedly was expelled for supporting Messali Hadj's claim that communists had been responsible for repressive measures taken against his *Etoile nord-africaine* Party, originally affiliated with the communists but frequently associated with *Ulema*, a pan-Arab movement.

safeguard what we have gained from one and the other, but let's reject the mystifications.'

That's how our discussion ended. Albert Camus, called away by numerous obligations, couldn't spare us any more of his time. But, as Lazarevich emphasized, that long hour of discussion would not be lost, and we hoped that there would be similar experiments in the future.

Lazarevich gives us his impression of that interview, which unfortunately did not recur:

Some of the others have tried to evoke Camus in the shop. I'm going to try to bring him back — undoubtedly it will be quite pale and lackluster, but I have to try, I really want to — to bring him back as he was for several short hours during the meeting of a study group created by our union. Imagine him as he was then — deliberately not at the speaker's platform but at a table, where we tried to communicate with one another during the meeting. I've forgotten the month and the year, but it doesn't matter; now that he's dead, everything is related. It all blends into a whole.

Camus still had his illusions about unions. He was unaware of the cancer of gross materialism in the unions, and he chose to look only at the good side of things. He saw us better than we are. We were better at that particular moment, pretty much because of him, because we wanted to be simple and real, sort of the way he wanted it. How far away at that moment were our worries about a good salary and what make of automobile we should buy; how remote was our vision of a refrigerator and of status acquired or to be acquired with the boss, our scheming to be recognized as 'qualified.'

All that was forgotten. We had Camus in front of us. Some of us had read his books, others had merely heard about them. A few, as has been mentioned earlier, worked at his side in the composing room. We found him simple, real, without false modesty, not a demagogue — yes, he had been real. Indeed, that's how he was then at the meeting, in that dimly lit hall with dirty windowpanes and the smell of two or three hundred men. We all wore our masks of 'proper men,' but once things began we were transformed a bit — politics and everyday problems were forgotten.

Camus was coming back to us. We had seen him leave, go to accept the Nobel Prize. We had seen him in newspaper photos; the flashbulbs had even shown him having a fling with members of high society, and our hearts were heavy — were they going to keep him? No, he had come back. The bourgeoisie hadn't killed him. He was among us, with his calm smile — a little ironic, but kind, friendly, telling us not to be sentimental but to know how to be close, to be brothers. We crowded around him for a couple of minutes before anyone spoke. Each of us would have liked to take him aside and renew his personal memory with Camus. But we weren't jealous, we couldn't be, because he was with us.

Then we began to communicate, precisely because of our agonizing concern for the truth. Here our thoughts ran along the same lines: we, proofreaders paid to 'proofread' lies, dress them up grammatically, and keep them from being awkward, and he, who had been able to make the bourgeoisie retreat, even to the point of thinking — to compel it by exposure to high ideals to confess, to see itself as it really was, to get inspired, to publish and disseminate the rejection of falsehood.

It began with Camus' refusal to read a prepared speech, to refer even to notes, or to begin a discourse. No, he didn't at all want to give us a tirade. There wasn't the slightest sign of affectation, nor of that pride which may be hidden but which resides, at least to some extent, in every man's soul. He was waiting for our questions, and they came — with a desire to know all and a sensitive concern to avoid offending him or infringing on his 'right of silence.' He had his smile, his best one, and he said something like this: 'Since we've agreed that

56

you can ask me everything and that I have the right to tell you all or refuse to answer, let's start.'

The first question concerned the problem of the reception of *The Just Assassins*. One of us said he was upset because that play, a vibrant treatment of the problem of murder in our times, hadn't made a stronger impression on the average man.

Camus assured us *The Just Assassins* had nevertheless been understood, but he wanted us to know that he was bitter when the story about the barrelmakers' strike, the outstanding one in *Exile and the Kingdom*, hadn't been reprinted by a single labor review. We tried to explain this by the constraint imposed by copyright laws, but he wouldn't accept that explanation — the reasons weren't economic. Bourgeois publishers were willing, but the labor editors were blind, deaf, and dumb — unintentionally, they hadn't noticed what was in that piece.

Then those encounters at the composing stone were brought up again. This time we saw our work in a different light. We had been near-sighted. We had only been aware of the haste, the exclamations, the making-up of the pages, the rough outbursts like, 'Oh, you mean he still hasn't kicked the bucket!' in reference to a dying celebrity whose obituary had been ready for a week and whose memory only furnished a pretext for discussing the merit of various kinds of type faces. But there was more to it than that. Camus reminded us of those moments, brief as they were, when we exchanged ideas. These were triggered by a concern for graphic beauty, which led suddenly to reflection. We could almost see again the heads of the worker and the writer, bent over a page that was still in type.

He told us he loved those moments, that this kind of work seemed less of a strain to him than writing. Then, seeing a look of incomprehension in our eyes — 'How could that be, Camus, when the book is merely being born?' — Camus told us that he wasn't a pretty sight at that moment, that 'you would have said that I was a nothing, a dunce pacing back and forth in his room.' But we knew that he didn't really know how he looked. We were there at that moment, invisible for him, and we saw how beautiful that pain was, how blessed it was, how the tormented flesh of his body was going to relax. The book would be born — we were certain of it — and it would be great. As far as we were concerned, Camus could pace from wall to wall; on those walls and next to us, a portrait of Tolstoy would be watching him. I believe this was the only picture, or one of the few, in his room — 'That's my father,' he had said.

He also told us that a writer ought to have two occuaptions, one for earning his daily bread and, the other, the real and absolute one, where he didn't have to cater to public taste and the only worry was not to lie to himself, above all in this thoughts, but also in the way he expressed those thoughts.

Once again we were helping one another. We had become petty, meticulous, and finicky from continually hunting for mistakes in the copy. He told us, however, that he had known several of us whose human dignity hadn't been completely stifled by the pettiness of the work. He said that some of us had helped him avoid making ugly mistakes, and he thanked them from the bottom of his heart. He indicated that there were some who were an even match for him when it came to discussion. Although they had parted without reaching agreement, he was grateful to them for showing him how much unexplored territory there still was in the most settled areas of knowledge. He also had sensed, unhappily, as we had ourselves, our pedantic side, the petty and mean pride we took in tracking down mistakes. One man, who had in mind that great show of grouchiness — but not rebellion — which gives a carnival atmosphere to our profession, has even called us 'anarchist pedants.'[1] Camus didn't say and never would say that.

A show-off who considered himself a Marxist tried to trip

1. As is apparent from the text of this book, there were and are proofreaders in France thoroughly dedicated to anarchist principles.

up Camus by asking him in what ways he thought a writer could serve as a guide to the proletariat. Our friend Camus answered simply that he had never been a guide, that he couldn't dream of being one, and that he felt too much real humility to put himself in the place of a multitude.

At the same time Camus had too many illusions about the nobility of the 'anarchist' ideal, which he mentally associated with those exceptional men who had actually lived out the life of 'the rebel.' The term 'anarchist pedant' would have sounded too much like a condemnation in the ears of Camus, who had in mind men who reach upwards for 'grace' but are too quickly brought down to earth by 'gravity,' as Simone Weil,[1] whom he thought about so much, would have said.

As far as we're concerned, we want to think about him. We want to be true to him, for his sake. We want men, when they think of that heap of scrap iron piled up against a tree not far from the Yonne[2] to hate that absurd death. But not every death is absurd.

Rarely, of course, can you choose your own death, but we can say that Camus knew how to choose his life. And that's what calls to us from beyond the absurdity of his death. One of Camus' statements (taken from a letter of March 19, 1956) survives through all of this: 'You don't ask murderers to rehabilitate the victim. Bulganin, Khrushchev, and the others are accomplices and nothing more.'[3]

In this age where hangmen triumph, Camus, or perhaps we should say the flesh-and-blood Camus, is no longer here. He was no more able than we to prevent that triumph and its

1. See Simone Weil, *The Need for Roots*, The Beacon Press, 1960.
2. See note 2. p 17.
3. The reference is to Khrushchev's and other Soviet leaders' decision to 're-habilitate,' after the Twentieth Party Congress of 1956, thousands of victims of the purges of the later 1930's. Khrushchev and Bulganin, of course, were important party officials at the time of these purges, for which they must share the responsibility.

very frequent recurrence. But his ideas endure, stronger and more alive than ever. It's up to us, and us alone, whether we will join with those 'others,' with those 'accomplices.' In a way it's a question of whether we are going to be faithful to what is eternal in Camus.

Albert Camus, born in Mondovi Algeria
7 November 1913
Died at Villeblevin France
4 January 1960

General Leclerc's division in Paris, 1944.

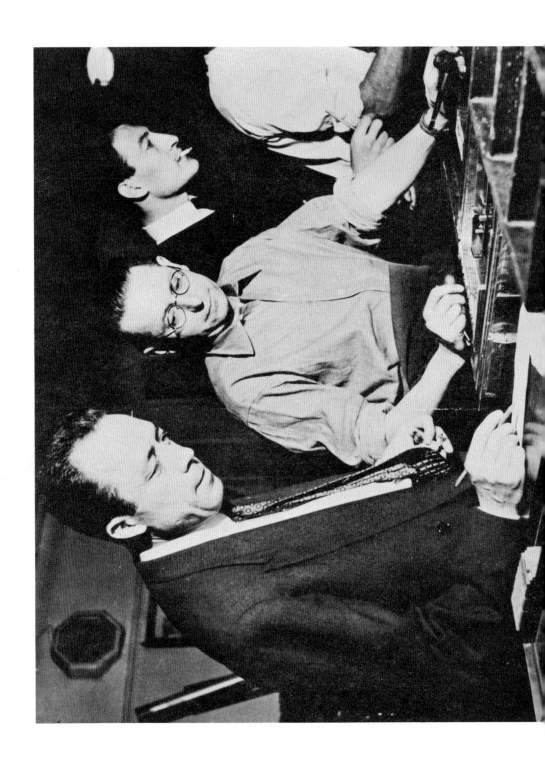

Camus at the stone, *Express*, 1955.

Printer's Note

The traditional expressions in the printing-typographic profession are rich in metaphors, for there are many craft secrets which can be recognized only by the initiates.

In the title of this book, *Albert Camus and the Men of the Stone*, the word 'Stone' describes a smooth marble surface for the imposition of type forms that are *made-ready* before it enters the *bed* or *putting to bed* in the printing press. Joseph Moxon* states, 'This *Stone* is to be laid upon a strong *Oaken*-wood Frame, made like the Frame of a common table, so high, that the Face of the *Stone* may lye about three Foot and an Inch above the Floor . . .'. It is here where the *stone hands* (compositors) prepare or *dress* the type forms, making sure that the imposition of the type pages are correctly in order. Usually, it is the meeting place where the men gather *around the stone* to discuss or exchange words. Today, metal imposing surfaces are commonly used throughout the printing trades, but they are still referred to colloquially by the old name: *the Stone*.

The text has been set by Othmar Peters of Peters Typesetting, Inc., in Monotype Bembo, a type based on designs by the Venetian, Francesco Griffo, whose types were used by Aldus Manutius at the beginning of the 16th century. The display type is Hunt Roman, designed by Hermann Zapf in 1962. Letterpress by Arlen Philpott; photo lithography by George Waters; binding by the Schuberth Bookbindery.

The typographic design and production of this book has been prepared by the publisher-typographer at the Greenwood Press, San Francisco, California. 750 copies have been printed in June 1971.

Jack Werner Stauffacher

Mechanick Exercises by Joseph Moxon, London 1683. Reprinted: Oxford University Press, Oxford, 1966.

Books by Albert Camus
translated into English.

The Stranger. New York: Knopf, 1946.
The Plague. New York: Knopf, 1948.
The Rebel: An Essay on Man in Revolt. New York: Knopf,
   1954.
The Myth of Sisyphus and Other Essays. New York: Knopf,
   1955.
The Fall. New York: Knopf, 1957.
Exile & the Kingdom. New York: Knopf, 1958.
Caligula & Three Other Plays [Misunderstanding; State of
   Siege; Just Assassins]. New York: Knopf, 1958.
The Possessed, A Play in Three Parts. New York: Knopf, 1960.
Resistance, Rebellion & Death. New York: Knopf, 1961.
Notebooks: 1935-1942. New York: Knopf, 1963.
Notebooks: 1942-1951. New York: Knopf, 1965.
Lyrical & Critical Essays. New York: Knopf, 1968.
Neither Victims nor Executioners. Berkeley: World Without
   War Council, 1968.

Critical writings in English on works by Camus.

Bree, Germaine, ed. *Camus, A Collection of Critical Essays.*
   Englewood Cliffs: Prentice-Hall, Inc., 1962.
Douglas, Kenneth, ed. *Albert Camus* (Yale French Studies).
   New Haven: Yale University, 1960.
Thody, Philip. *Albert Camus, A Study of His Work.* New York:
   Grove Press Inc., 1957.
Cruickshank, John. *Albert Camus and the Literature of Revolt.*
   New York: Oxford University Press, 1960.
King, Adele. *Albert Camus.* New York: Grove Press, Inc.1964.
Parker, Emmett. *Albert Camus, The Artist in the Arena.*
   Madison, The University of Wisconsin Press, 1966.

O'Brien, Conor Cruise. *Albert Camus of Europe and Africa.*
New York: The Viking Press, 1970.

Hoy, Peter. *Camus in English* (an annotated Bibliography of
Albert Camus's contribution to English and American
Periodicals and Newspapers). Leicestershire: Brewhouse
Press, 1968 (private printing, 250 copies).

CREDITS

Madame Camus: pp. 35, 62.   René-Saint Paul: pp. 15, 36, 41;
Télé Photo: p. 29;   Cartier Bresson–Magnum: p. 47;
Papillon photo: p. 42 (from *à Paris sous la botte des Nazis,*
Editions Raymond Schall, Paris, 1944);
Library of Contemporary International Documentation, Paris: p. 30;
Newspaper Collection, Hoover Institution on War, Revolution,
and Peace, Stanford University: p. 48.